# Drawing and Learning About Cats

**Using Shapes and Lines**

written and illustrated by
Amy Bailey Muehlenhardt

Thanks to our advisers for their expertise, research, and advice:

Linda Frichtel, Design Adjunct Faculty, MCAD
Minneapolis, Minnesota

Susan Kesselring, M.A., Literacy Educator
Rosemount–Apple Valley–Eagan (Minnesota) School District

PICTURE WINDOW BOOKS
Minneapolis, Minnesota

**Amy Bailey Muehlenhardt** grew up in Fergus Falls, Minnesota, and attended Minnesota State University in Moorhead. She holds a Bachelor of Science degree in Graphic Design and Art Education. Before coming to Picture Window Books, Amy was an elementary art teacher. She always impressed upon her students that "everyone is an artist." Amy lives in Mankato, Minnesota, with her husband, Brad, and daughter, Elise.

For Elise Lauren, my new smile.
ABM

Editorial Director: Carol Jones
Managing Editor: Catherine Neitge
Creative Director: Keith Griffin
Editor: Jill Kalz
Editorial Adviser: Bob Temple
Story Consultant: Terry Flaherty
Designer: Jaime Martens
Page Production: Picture Window Books
The illustrations in this book were created with pencil and colored pencil.

Picture Window Books
5115 Excelsior Boulevard
Suite 232
Minneapolis, MN 55416
1-877-845-8392
www.picturewindowbooks.com

Copyright © 2006 by Picture Window Books
All rights reserved. No part of this book may be reproduced without written permission from the publisher. The publisher takes no responsibility for the use of any of the materials or methods described in this book, nor for the products thereof.

Printed in the United States of America.

**Library of Congress Cataloging-in-Publication Data**
Muehlenhardt, Amy Bailey, 1974–
Drawing and learning about cats / written and illustrated by Amy Bailey Muehlenhardt.
p. cm. — (Sketch it!)
Includes bibliographical references and index.
ISBN 1-4048-1190-7 (hardcover)
1. Cats in art—Juvenile literature. 2. Drawing—Technique—Juvenile literature. I. Title: Cats. II. Title.
NC783.8.C36M84 2005
743.6'9752—dc22     2005007171

# Table of Contents

Everyone Is an Artist . . . . . . . . . . . . . . . 4
American Shorthair . . . . . . . . . . . . . . 8
Siamese . . . . . . . . . . . . . . . . . . . . . . 10
Burmese . . . . . . . . . . . . . . . . . . . . . 12
Siberian . . . . . . . . . . . . . . . . . . . . . 14
Cornish Rex . . . . . . . . . . . . . . . . . . 16
Persian . . . . . . . . . . . . . . . . . . . . . . 18
Turkish Angora . . . . . . . . . . . . . . . 20
Sphynx . . . . . . . . . . . . . . . . . . . . . . 22
To Learn More . . . . . . . . . . . . . . . . 24

# Everyone Is an Artist
## There is no right or wrong way to draw!

With a little patience and some practice, anyone can learn to draw. Did you know every picture begins as a simple shape? If you can draw shapes, you can draw anything.

## The Basics of Drawing

**line**—a long mark made by a pen, a pencil, or another tool

**guideline**—a line used to help you draw; the guideline will be erased when your drawing is almost complete

**shade**—to color in with your pencil

**value**—the lightness or darkness of an object

**shape**—the form or outline of an object or figure

**diagonal**—a shape or line that leans to the side

# Before you begin, you will need

a pencil,
an eraser,
lots of paper!

## Four Tips for Drawing

### 1. Draw very lightly.
Try drawing light, medium, and dark lines. The softer you press, the lighter the lines will be.

### 2. Draw your shapes.
When you are finished drawing, connect your shapes with a sketch line.

### 3. Add details.
Details are small things that make a good picture even better.

### 4. Color your art.
Use your colored pencils, crayons, or markers to create backgrounds.

# Let's get started!

# Simple shapes help you draw.
Practice drawing these shapes before you begin.

 **circle**
A circle is round like a ball.

 **triangle**
A triangle has three sides and three corners.

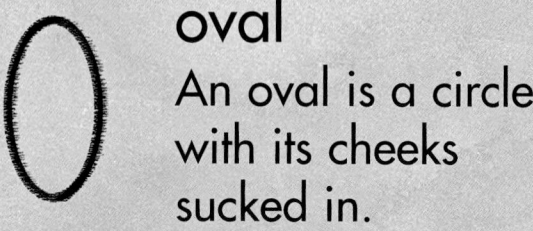 **oval**
An oval is a circle with its cheeks sucked in.

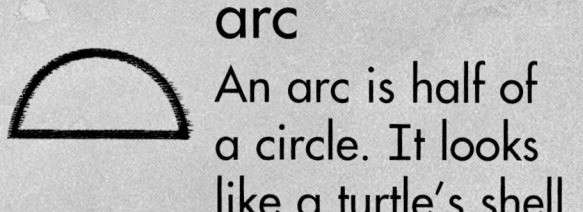 **arc**
An arc is half of a circle. It looks like a turtle's shell.

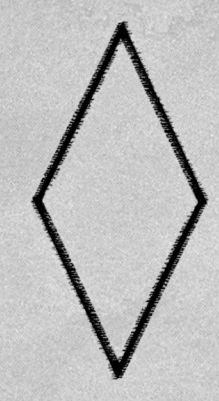 **diamond**
A diamond is two triangles put together.

 **square**
A square has four equal sides and four corners.

 **trapezoid**
A trapezoid has four sides and four corners. Two of its sides are different lengths.

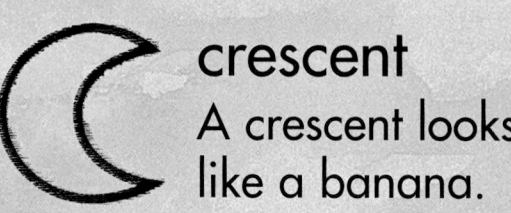 **crescent**
A crescent looks like a banana.

 **rectangle**
A rectangle has two long sides, two short sides, and four corners.

# You will also use lines when drawing.
Practice drawing these lines.

| **vertical**
A vertical line stands tall like a tree.

 **zigzag**
A zigzag line is sharp and pointy.

— **horizontal**
A horizontal line lies down and takes a nap.

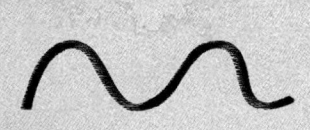 **wavy**
A wavy line moves up and down like a roller coaster.

 **diagonal**
A diagonal line leans to the side.

**Remember to practice drawing.**

While using this book, you may want to stop drawing at step five or six. That's great! Everyone is at a different drawing level.

Don't worry if your picture isn't perfect. The important thing is to have fun.

**dizzy**
A dizzy line spins around and around.

# Be creative!

# American Shorthair

The American Shorthair is one of the most common cats in the world. It's easy to care for, friendly, and very healthy. Most American Shorthairs are silver with black markings, but they can be many other colors.

## Step 1
Draw an arc for the body and a circle for the head.

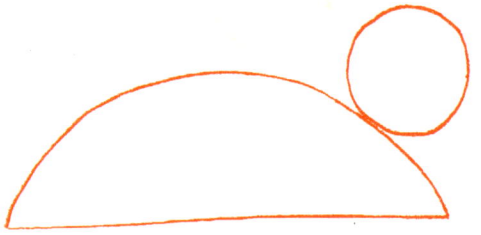

## Step 2
Draw a circle for the muzzle. Add two triangles for the ears and a curved line for the tail.

## Step 3
Draw two circles for the eyes and a triangle for the nose.

## Step 4
Draw six ovals for the legs. Draw three ovals for the paws. The fourth leg and paw are hiding.

## Step 5

Define the cat with a sketch line. Add two curved lines for the mouth.

## Step 6

Erase the extra lines. Add details such as stripes, pupils, whiskers, and toes.

## Step 7

Color your cat and add a background.

# Siamese

Its deep blue eyes make the Siamese cat a favorite among cat lovers. Its long, angled body and sharp chin give it a royal look. The Siamese cat is friendly and smart, and its silky fur makes it great to snuggle with.

### Step 1
Draw two circles for the body.

### Step 2
Draw a circle for the head and two triangles for the ears.

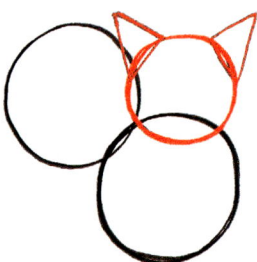

### Step 3
Draw a circle for the muzzle. Add two circles for the eyes and a triangle for the nose.

### Step 4
Draw three curved lines for the legs. The fourth leg is hiding.

## Step 5

Draw a curved line for the tail. Add two ovals for the pupils. Define the cat with a sketch line.

## Step 6

Erase the extra lines. Add details such as whiskers and a mouth.

## Step 7

Color your cat and add a background.

# Burmese

Some people say the Burmese looks like a "brick wrapped in silk" because of its sturdy body and soft fur. The Burmese is full of energy and often mischievous. It also loves being around people.

## Step 1
Draw an oval for the body and a circle for the head.

## Step 2
Draw circles for the eyes and muzzle. Add two triangles for the ears and one for the nose.

## Step 3
Draw two ovals for the hind legs and two for the paws. Add a curved line for the tail.

## Step 4
Draw two curved lines for the front legs and paws.

## Step 5

Define the cat with a sketch line. Add two curved lines for the mouth and one for the chin.

## Step 6

Erase the extra lines. Add details such as whiskers and toes.

## Step 7

Color your cat and add a background.

# Siberian

The Siberian cat is energetic and full of surprises. Its glaring eyes and pointed ears make it seem dangerous. But it loves to play and can jump great distances.

## Step 1
Draw a circle for the head and an oval for the body.

## Step 2
Add two triangles for the ears. Draw an oval for the muzzle.

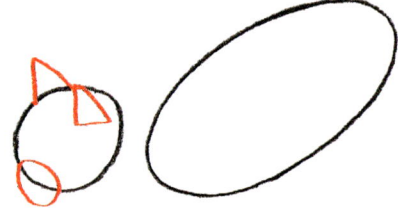

## Step 3
Draw an oval for the eye. Add a triangle for the nose. Draw two curved lines for the neck.

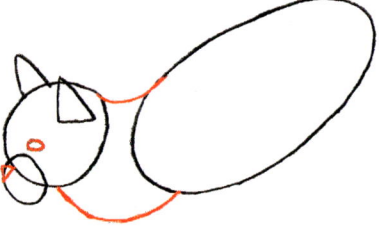

## Step 4
Draw nine ovals for the legs and paws.

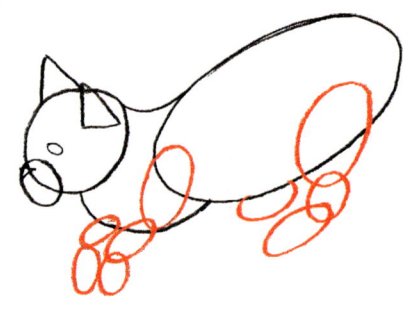

## Step 5

Draw a curved line for the tail. Define the cat with a zigzag sketch line.

## Step 6

Erase the extra lines. Add details such as a pupil, whiskers, toes, and fur.

## Step 7

Color your cat and add a background.

# Cornish Rex

The Cornish Rex looks like it's from another world. Big eyes, curly fur, and huge ears give it a unique look. And you won't be able to tell its age by the way it acts—a Cornish Rex will act like a kitten its whole life!

### Step 1
Draw an oval and a circle for the body.

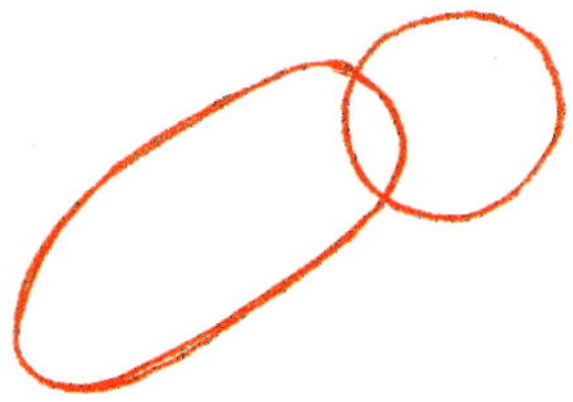

### Step 2
Draw a circle for the head and two curved lines for the neck.

### Step 3
Add two triangles for the ears. Draw two circles for the eyes and a triangle for the nose.

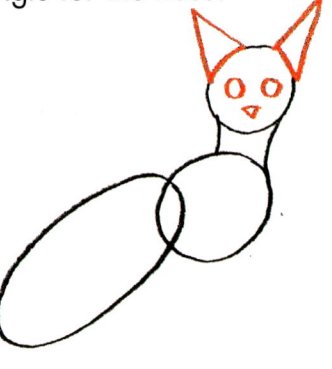

### Step 4
Draw four ovals and three rectangles for the legs. Add three circles and one oval for the paws.

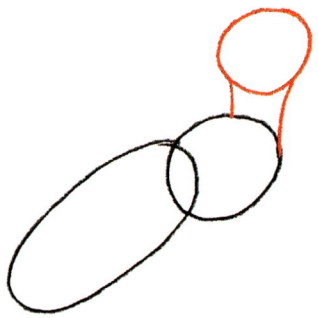

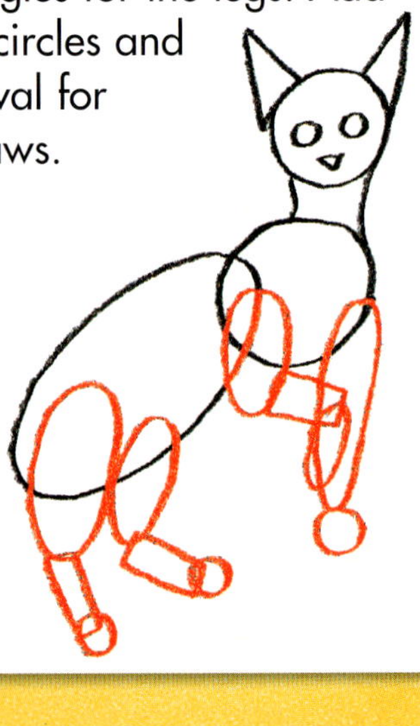

## Step 5

Draw a crescent for the tail. Define the cat with a wavy sketch line.

## Step 6

Erase the extra lines. Add details such as whiskers, pupils, and color patches.

## Step 7

Color your cat and add a background.

# Persian

A fluffy white coat makes the Persian cat stand out from other cats. The Persian cat is sweet and gentle. Its short ears and big eyes make it look frightened, but as long as it feels comfortable and secure, it's happy.

## Step 1
Draw a small circle inside a large circle for the body and the head.

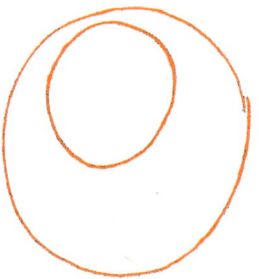

## Step 2
Add two triangles for the ears. Draw two ovals for the eyes.

## Step 3
Draw two ovals for the chest and one for the tail.

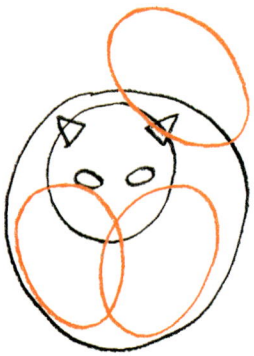

## Step 4
Draw three rectangles for the legs and three for the paws. The fourth leg and paw are hiding.

## Step 5

Define the cat with a zigzag sketch line. Add a triangle for the nose and two curved lines for the mouth.

## Step 6

Erase the extra lines. Add details such as pupils and fur.

## Step 7

Color your cat and add a background.

# Turkish Angora

A graceful, intelligent cat, the Turkish Angora was once thought to be extinct. It has a thin, smooth body with medium-length fur and a long, puffy tail. It shows great love for its owners and enjoys running and playing.

## Step 1
Draw a circle and an oval for the body.

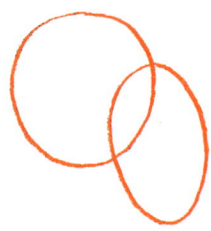

## Step 2
Draw a circle for the head and two triangles for the ears.

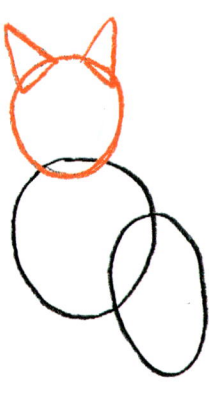

## Step 3
Draw a circle for the muzzle. Draw two ovals for the eyes and a triangle for the nose.

## Step 4
Draw six rectangles for the legs. The fourth leg is hiding. Add a curved line for the tail.

## Step 5

Define the cat with a zigzag sketch line. Add three curved lines for the mouth.

## Step 6

Erase the extra lines. Add details such as pupils, whiskers, and fur.

## Step 7

Color your cat and add a background.

# Sphynx

A hairless cat? Well, not totally. The sphynx has fine hair on its nose and sometimes on its body. With so little hair, the sphynx is good at finding cozy places in which to curl up and keep warm.

## Step 1
Draw one circle and one oval for the body.

## Step 2
Draw one circle for the head and one for the muzzle.

## Step 3
Draw two ovals for the eyes. Draw two large triangles for the ears. Add a triangle for the nose.

## Step 4
Draw five rectangles for the legs and paws. The fourth leg and paw are hiding.

## Step 5

Define the cat with a sketch line. Draw three curved lines for the mouth. Add a crescent for the tail.

## Step 6

Erase the extra lines. Add details such as spots and short, curved lines for the wrinkles.

## Step 7

Color your cat and add a background.

23

# To Learn More

## At the Library

Bratun, Katy. *Drawing Cats*. New York: Grosset & Dunlap, 2002.

Doering, Amanda. *Cats ABC: An Alphabet Book*. Mankato, Minn.: A+ Books, 2005.

Meyer, Ted. *Cats Around the World*. Santa Monica, Calif.: Santa Monica Press, 2003.

Waters, Jo. *The Wild Side of Pet Cats*. Chicago: Raintree Publishing, 2005.

## On the Web

### FactHound

FactHound offers a safe, fun way to find Web sites related to this book. All of the sites on FactHound have been researched by our staff.

*http://www.facthound.com*

1. Visit the FactHound home page.
2. Enter a search word related to this book, or type in this special code: 1404811907.
3. Click on the FETCH IT button.

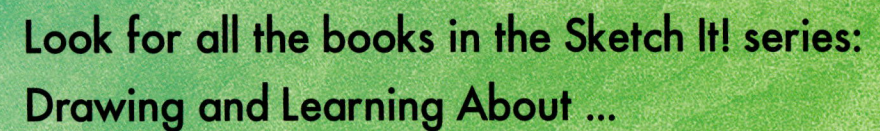

Your trusty FactHound will fetch the best sites for you!

## Look for all the books in the Sketch It! series:
## Drawing and Learning About ...

| | | |
|---|---|---|
| Bugs | Faces | Monsters |
| Cars | Fashion | Monster Trucks |
| Cats | Fish | |
| Dinosaurs | Horses | |
| Dogs | Jungle Animals | |